Contents

Britain's Got Talent 2010 Intro 6

The Auditions Intro 8

The Auditions 10

Semi-Final Intro 26

Semi-Final 1 28

Semi-Final 2 32

Semi-Final 3 36

Semi-Final 4 40

Semi-Final 5 44

The Finalists 48

Liam McNally 50

Janey Cutler 54

Christopher Stone 58

Paul Burling 62

Connected 66

Tina & Chandi 70

Tobias Mead 74

Kieran Gaffney 78

Twist & Pulse 84

Spelbound 90

Series 1 – Memorable Moments 98

Series 2 – Memorable Moments 100

Series 3 – Memorable Moments 102

Series 3 Runner-Up – Susan Boyle 104

Series 3 Winner – Diversity 106

Winner 2011 108

BRITAIN'S GOT TALENT

Pedigree®

Written by Rachel Elliot.
Published 2010. Pedigree Books, Beech Hill House,
Walnut Gardens, Exeter, Devon, EX4 4DH.
books@pedigreegroup.co.uk • www.pedigreebooks.com

£7.99

BR

T

2 0

Welcome to a celebration of the show where talent makes **dreams come true!** The UK's favourite **fun-filled** talent show has introduced some of the most impressive, moving and hilarious acts in the country, leading up to a **sparkling grand final.**

The show is open to any performer of any age from any background, and that means that if you **believe in yourself**, anything is possible! The winner's wonderful prize is £100,000 and an appearance on the Royal Variety Performance.

TAIN'S GOT ENT 1 0

Remind yourself of the highlights and memorable moments of this fantastic series, and enjoy your favourite acts all over again. This is your turn to judge the Judges and get the low-down on all the amazing and unforgettable finalists.

From **dancing dogs** to **guitarists on pogo sticks**, from Cardiff to Glasgow, the talent just keeps on coming. Follow the drama and excitement from the auditions to the Live Grand Final, and relive the only show that's jam-packed with the **best talent** and the **biggest dreams** in Britain!

THE AUDITIONS

Wild, weird and wonderful, nothing quite compares to the craziness of the *Britain's Got Talent* auditions!

This year, the Judges travel to Glasgow, Manchester, Cardiff, Newcastle, Birmingham and London, seeking acts that are good enough to compete for a place at the Royal Variety Performance.

GLASGOW

NEWCASTLE

MANCHESTER

BIRMINGHAM

CARDIFF

LONDON

SIMON   AMANDA   PIERS

The atmosphere is electric! The audience is here, fizzing with excitement as they take their seats. Ant and Dec are here, ready to introduce a fun-filled show for the viewers at home. The performers are here, waiting anxiously backstage for their shot at stardom. And of course the Judges are here, keen to start the auditions and find out what talents Britain has to offer in 2010.

Who will be the first to walk onto that stage? Will it be a potential winner? The audience is waiting, the Judges are waiting and the three red buzzers are waiting.

BRITAIN'S GOT TALENT 2010 IS ABOUT TO BEGIN!

AUDITIONS ★ ★ ★ ★ ★ ★ ★
SUPER GROUPS
HIGHLIGHTS

TEAM SHAOLIN
This team's martial art is an ancient form of Kung-fu. Their moves include two-finger handstands!

THE CHEEKY BOYS
The Cheeky Boys' balloon act gets three buzzers.

"What would happen if those balloons burst?"

"That was so exciting!"

"That was genius!"

THE CHIPPENDOUBLES
These dancing lookalikes are great fun, and the audience loves every minute of their routine.

A3
These three brothers from Swansea love performing together.

TAP ATTACK
These dancing girls hope to tap their way to the Royal Variety Performance.

"You're exceptionally talented!"

"IT'S ALWAYS WORTHWHILE COMING HERE."

"I'D LIKE TO THINK THAT NEWCASTLE CAN PRODUCE BETTER TALENT THAN ANT AND DEC!"

TRINITY WARRIORS

This male breakdancing troupe are a breath of fresh air onstage and the Judges love their performance.

THE THREE MORPHATEERS

The coloured body stockings don't win the Judges' approval and the performance gets three nos.

PERIDOT

The nine members of Peridot are passionate about street dance and have been together for four years.

"I love your enthusiasm."

"I think you're very dangerous and compelling to watch."

HAYASHI

A blindfold Samurai sword act grabs Simon's attention!

"Great energy and brilliant performance."

THREEBEE

These Bollywood dancers light up the stage with their passion for dance.

11

AUDITIONS
SUPER GROUPS
HIGHLIGHTS

"A brilliant idea."

THE GAFFNEY FAMILY
Kieran Gaffney returns to the stage with his family after missing out on a place in the semi-finals last year.

"You were fantastic."

THE ARRANGEMENT
This unusual group give modern music a classical twist.

"Beautiful chaos."

"You were a treat."

TABOO
It's obvious that these young dancers love performing.

VANESSA MILLAR DANCE SCHOOL
The girls swallow their nerves and give an energetic can-can routine in lavish costumes.

DANCE FLAVOURZ
These Brazilian dancers sizzle onstage and get the audience and the Judges in the mood for dancing.

"You are utterly compelling to watch."

12

RUBY GIRLS

These trained dancers are dedicated to performing.

"Very sassy!"

THE SIRENS

Three ambulance service workers from Norfolk give the Judges a surprise when they strip down to leotards!

"It was all a good laugh."

AKA

The dance group hope to make Newcastle proud and show that the North East has talent.

"We're a crowd-pleaser!"

MYZTIKAL

A dance troupe with a twist - they sing as well as dance!

STARBURST

These pint-sized dancers are bursting with energy and excitement.

"Fun, cute, brilliant!"

"The twist was great."

AUDITIONS
GOING SOLO
HIGHLIGHTS

JULIE WATKINS
Julie is a cleaner in a police station, but her dream is to perform onstage.

PAUL HUNN
'The Burper' has big dreams of getting to the Royal Variety Performance.

"I actually found it quite threatening."

"It's a repulsed 'no' from me!"

DAVID ATKINSON
David dreams of being in martial arts films like Bruce Lee. But the Judges were scared that he was going to hurt himself!

"There's something about you that is just mesmerising."

COREY SEAN
Corey is a self-taught dancer who can't wait to start entertaining the crowd.

BAT JACKSON
After his success as Darth Jackson, Philip Farrugia returns to the stage!

"clever but silly."

"I think you are great fun."

"I'M REALLY EXCITED ABOUT FINDING SOMETHING GREAT TODAY."

"DO WE HAVE A STAR?"

PIPPA THE RIPPER

The circus performer sails through to the next round.

DAVE LEVALLE

Dave's mother-in-law joke has the Judges reaching for their buzzers.

"The best I've ever seen anyone do that!"

"Dave, you definitely need new material!"

CONRAD BRISSETT

Conrad's inventive routine has the audience screaming in delight!

CHRISTINE WILKES

The Judges don't think the world is ready for Michael Jackson on the castanets!

"She needs to go on the naughty step."

"I'd love to see what else you've got."

"I haven't seen moonwalking that slow since Neil Armstrong!"

MATILDA

This stroppy pianist threw a tantrum when the Judges didn't appreciate her playing!

15

AUDITIONS
GOING SOLO
HIGHLIGHTS

KEVIN CRUISE
The entertainer of *The Fishy Rose* is a roaring success.

SINEAD
She thinks her pogo stick performance will make her stand out, but the Judges are not impressed.

"I would go cruising with you any time."

LHOURAII LI
Lhouraii's contemporary dance performance is very different but the Judges really like her.

"Jamie, what were you thinking?"

"That was just stupid!"

THE HARDINATOR
Jamie's purple body suit grabs the audience's attention, but his dancing doesn't.

SCOTT HARTSHORNE
Scott works in a clothes shop and dreams of performing onstage. But his dreams will have to wait a little longer – the Judges give him three nos.

72

JAMES AITCHENSON

The singing bodybuilder failed to impress the judges.

"The singing was pretty awful!"

SCOTT BARRATT

Scott hopes that he has a future as an entertainer.

"You can't sing and you can't dance!"

PATRICK MACDONAL

Patrick's spirit and enthusiasm are hugely entertaining.

"I like the fact that you're very proud of this country!"

EGG

MANUEL MARTINEZ

Manuel is a true variety act – a ventriloquist who mimes to the Bee Gees, Leona Lewis and Susan Boyle!

JEFF DERBYSHIRE

Jeff the skipping stripper surprised everyone!

"Speaking on behalf of the Royal Family, I'm going to say NO!"

17

AUDITIONS DOUBLE TIME
HIGHLIGHTS

"We're different people but the dream is the same."

60388

DIFFERENT DREAMS
Best friends Ruth and Chantelle share a big dream. But can their friendship survive the Judges' comments?

"You've waited twenty-five years for this moment!"

FATHER & SON
Graham and James enjoy writing and performing comedy sketches and songs together.

PIPES & BRUMS
Pipes and Brums made the Judges laugh – but that wasn't their intention!

"The best thing about the act was your weird faces."

PERSEPHONE LEWIN
A toy penguin, a trumpet and an inflating rubber glove. How can she go wrong?

"I WOULD ABSOLUTELY LOVE A VARIETY ACT TO WIN *BRITAIN'S GOT TALENT*."

"I'D LOVE TO FIND A REALLY, REALLY TALENTED DOG ACT."

TINA & CHANDI
One of the all-time favourite dog acts across all the series!

"Chandi is a star!"

EILEEN & NIP THE DOG
Eileen hopes that her cheeky sidekick will help her reach the Royal Variety Performance, but the Judges weren't interested.

"I'm afraid it's three no's!"

STAR
Star the pig gets an attack of stage fright!

"He didn't do a lot did he?"

DOUBLE TAKE
Candy and Cat have been playing the timbrel since they were children.

"Everything was wrong!"

19

AUDITIONS DOUBLE TIME
HIGHLIGHTS

ALI BABA
Kelsey and Memet's fusion of Michael Jackson and traditional Turkish dancing has the audience on the edge of its seat for all the wrong reasons.

PHOENIX DANCERS
The beautiful Phoenix Dancers know how to put on a show, and hope that the Judges will enjoy their routine.

POL AND DAZ
Pol and Daz's hope that their hilarious performance will bring them a little closer to their dream of stardom.

"I found that a bit desperate."

MICHAEL FAYOMBO SNR & JNR
A shared love of Michael Jackson brings this father and son act to the auditions.

"It shouldn't have worked but it did!"

"IT'S BRILLIANT TO BE BACK, WHO KNOWS WHAT WE'LL FIND TODAY?"

"WE JUST HAVE TO FIND ONE DECENT PERSON HERE."

THE BALLOON BROTHERS

Anything is possible with these masters of balloon art!

RICHARD & COCO

Coco the dog has some fabulous football skills, but Simon asks him to come back next year with a canine football team!

"Genius!"

"We call it streetomedy!"

LOUISE SINCLAIR & ALI

Louise Sinclair and Ali need a little more practice!

TWIST & PULSE

Glen and Ashley see the future opening up for them when their audition goes well.

JACK & KATY

Jack and Katy dance their hearts out, but is it enough to win three yesses from the Judges?

"I think Ali got a bit nervous!"

AUDITIONS OLD SCHOOL HIGHLIGHTS

MICHAEL LAVENDER
The animal impressionist lays an egg onstage!

96867

"It's the strangest act I've ever seen."

DAVID CHURCHER
David's angelic poetry reading didn't please the Judges in Birmingham.

50996

"Angels angels everywhere, one on my shoulder, one in my hair!"

73099

74796

"Very nice to meet you both"

PETER & DOREEN
The Judges admire their enthusiasm, but the singers still get three buzzers!

CLIFFORD FORD
Clifford's smart outfit impresses the Judges – but will his performance do the same?

97571

JAMES SHIELDS
James loves playing the clarinet and hopes to share the feeling it gives him with the Royal Variety Performance audience.

"When I play the clarinet I get a warm feeling inside."

★ **"I HAVE A FEELING GLASGOW WILL DELIVER THE GOODS AGAIN."** ★

★ **"THERE'S NO AGE LIMIT ON DREAMS."** ★

SEAN SHEEHAN
This unique acts combines wood chopping, singing and impersonating Sean Connery!

"Very neat chops on the wood!"

KAREN TIERNEY
Karen's wig doesn't transform her into Tina Turner for the Judges.

"Literally nothing happened!"

MAX & IRENE
Irene hopes to show the Judges that her parrot Max can feed himself mashed potato with a fork.

"He wasn't hungry."

DAVE THOMPSON
Dave would love to be as successful as Bob Monkhouse.

"That was just awful."

"I didn't expect a set of lungs like that!"

JANEY CUTLER
Janey's voice had the audience on their feet!

"You've definitely improved!"

PHILIP GRIMMER
Female impersonator Philip has moved on from copying Kylie to mimicking Madonna.

AUDITIONS
NEW SCHOOL
HIGHLIGHTS

MAX THE DOG
Max comes onstage to show off his dance skills, but stage fright gets the better of him!

"Every dog should have its day!"

TYLER PATTERSON
Tyler learned his moves from MTV videos.

"You didn't move your lips!"

"You're very, very talented."

JOSH BARRY
Josh has performed in the West End, but he dreams of the Royal Variety stage.

"That was a brilliant performance."

LEWIS & BOBBY
Ten-year-old ventriloquist Lewis gives a comic performance that really impresses the Judges.

"MANCHESTER IS ALWAYS FULL OF VERY, VERY ENTERTAINING PEOPLE."

"I DON'T KNOW WHAT TO EXPECT."

OLIVIA ARCHBOLD

This nervous young singer gives a dazzling performance and impresses the Judges.

JOSH WARNER CAMPBELL

The Judges are impressed with Josh's attitude and dance moves.

"I like you, Josh."

"I don't think you know how good you really are."

"You're all very cute."

CONNECTED

The youngest boy band on the block sing their hearts out!

BEN JONSON

This dancing magician dreams of performing in music videos and casts a spell over the Judges.

"You have real warmth."

LIAM McNALLY

Liam's passion for music shines through every note he sings.

"I think you've got potential."

25

THE SEMI-FINALS

The auditions are over and an almost impossible task faces the Judges. Together they have to choose just forty acts to go through to the live semi-finals. Whose hopes will be shattered and who will be one step closer to making their dreams come true?

The live semi-finals will showcase eight hopeful acts each night, and the audience can now vote for their favourites. The act with the most public votes will go through to the final, and the Judges will pick their favourite between the second and third-placed acts.

As Ant and Dec step forward to host a thrilling evening of drama and talent, the cheering audience is breathless with excitement.

Backstage, nerves jangle and opportunities shimmer in the mind's eye. It's not enough for the semi-finalists to perform their audition piece again – they have to present something spectacular to make their dreams come true.

Who will rise to the challenge and be the best of the best?

SEMI FINAL 1

Olivia Archbold

Kevin Cruise

Threebee

Sean Sheehan

Stevie Starr

Josh Barry

Spelbound

Tobias Mead

Taboo

Neil Fullard

Kev Orkian

Michael Fayombo
Snr & Jnr

SEMI FINAL2

Maxxie Oliver

Ruby Girls

Tina & Chandi

Connected

SEMI FINAL3

Starburst

Chloe Hickinbottom

Jimmy Forde

Peridot

The Arrangement

Philip Grimmer

Paul Burling

Christopher Stone

Ice

Tyler Patterson

Emile Harris

Team Shaolin

Janey Cutler

Twist & Pulse

The Fusion

Mark James

SEMI FINAL4

SEMI FINAL5

The Chippendoubles

Myztikal

A3

Liam McNally

Alesia Vazmitsel

Dance Flavourz

Father & Son

Kieran Gaffney

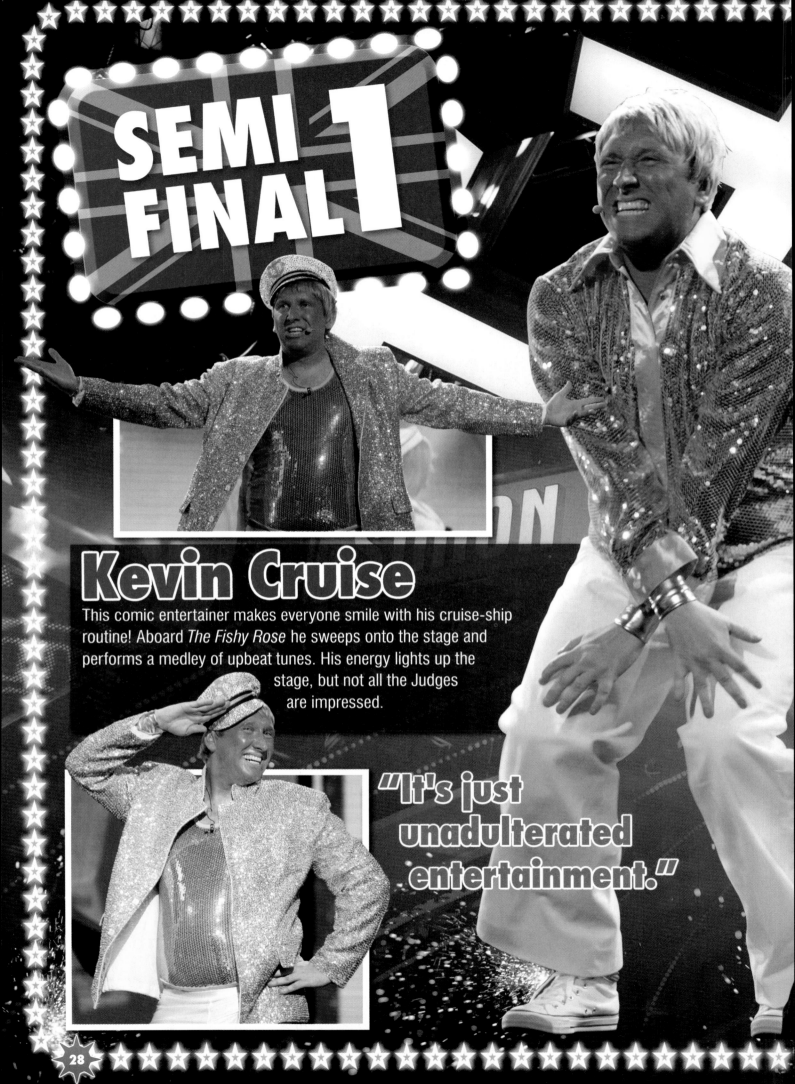

SEMI FINAL 1

Kevin Cruise

This comic entertainer makes everyone smile with his cruise-ship routine! Aboard *The Fishy Rose* he sweeps onto the stage and performs a medley of upbeat tunes. His energy lights up the stage, but not all the Judges are impressed.

"It's just unadulterated entertainment."

Josh Berry

Sixteen-year-old Josh Berry is a student who dreams of being a professional singer. The audience love him, and it's obvious that Josh feels he belongs on the stage. But can he persuade the Judges that he deserves a place in the glittering final?

"You were born to do it."

Olivia Archbold

Olivia is just fourteen-years-old, but her spellbinding voice is worthy of a place in the semi-finals. She is singing for her grandmother, who passed away in 2009. This inspiration lends soul and depth to her voice, and the audience responds to the emotion with warmth and praise. Olivia proves that she has superstar potential!

"You should feel very proud of yourself."

SEMI FINAL 1

Stevie Starr

Stevie Starr, otherwise known as the Regurgitator, shocks the audience by swallowing Amanda's engagement ring! He then swallows a locked padlock, unlocks it in his stomach, attaches the key to it, locks it and regurgitates it. How does he do it? And is this an act fit for the Royal Variety Performance?

"It is astonishing what you do."

Sean Sheehan

Sean Sheehan is the King of Kindling and a singing Sean Connery impersonator. He hopes that his act will get the UK chopping kindling and singing his song! However, his speedy chopping earns him two buzzers from Simon and Amanda.

"Dangerous and unpredictable."

Threebee

This Bollywood dance troupe opens the semi-finals with a passionate, show-stopping number that delights the audience and has the Judges singing their praises. Their creativity, energy and enthusiasm shine through and make a spectacular opening to the show!

"It was an energetic, colourful, fabulous start to the show"

Tobias Mead

THROUGH TO THE FINAL

Spelbound

SEMI FINAL 2

Maxxie Oliver

Maxxie descends to the stage in a dramatic costume, balancing precariously on a gigantic yellow phone! He writhes, shimmies and dazzles in true Lady Gaga style, but can his singing match his outfit? The Judges are unimpressed . . .

"I don't know what to say."

Michael Fayombo Snr & Jnr

This father and son act present a unique Michael Jackson tribute – a whirling concoction of moonwalking, crotch-grabbing and stylish moves. But the Judges aren't as impressed as they were in the audition. The Fayombos will have to depend on the audience vote!

"It's become embarrassing."

Neil Fullard

Unassuming doorman Neil Fullard has always loved singing, but he has never had the nerve to do anything about it – until now. He would love to earn a living through singing. As his friends say, it's better than standing out in the freezing cold! Neil takes command of the stage in a stylish tuxedo, singing a popular Frank Sinatra number. He looks as if he was born to be on stage!

"I thought you were absolutely fantastic."

33

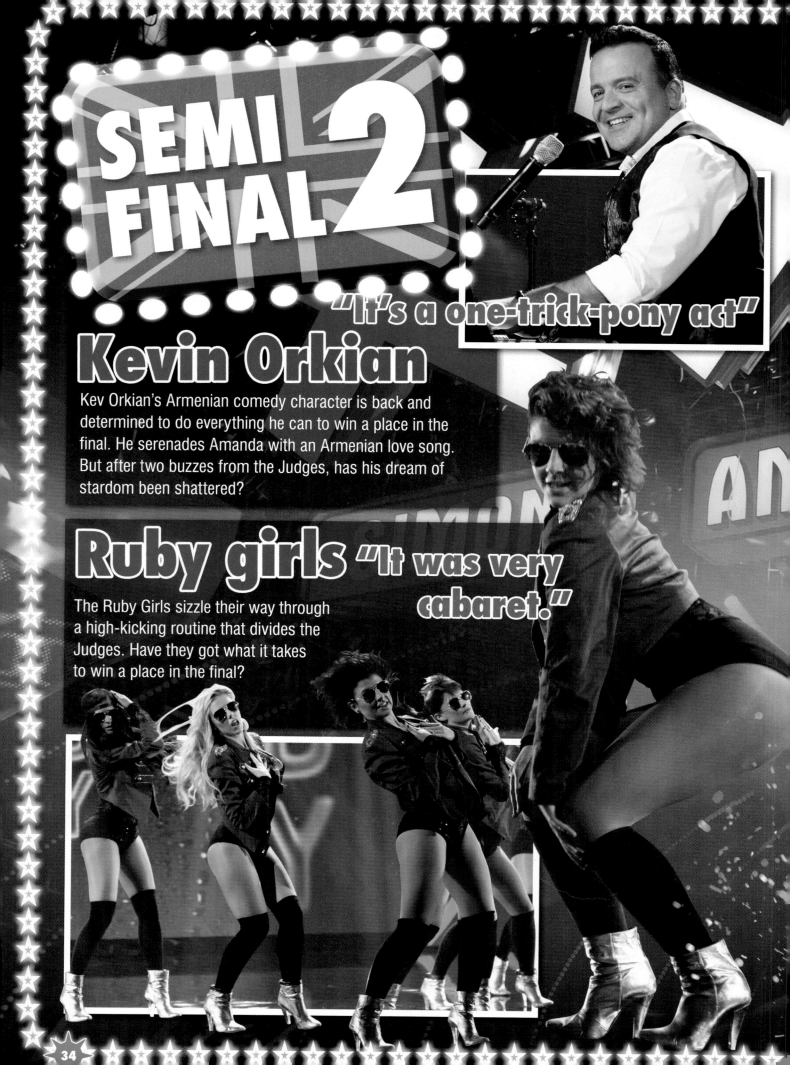

SEMI FINAL 2

"It's a one-trick-pony act"

Kevin Orkian

Kev Orkian's Armenian comedy character is back and determined to do everything he can to win a place in the final. He serenades Amanda with an Armenian love song. But after two buzzes from the Judges, has his dream of stardom been shattered?

Ruby girls "It was very cabaret."

The Ruby Girls sizzle their way through a high-kicking routine that divides the Judges. Have they got what it takes to win a place in the final?

Taboo

Taboo bursts into the spotlights with a candy-themed routine. Dressed in red and white and dancing around two giant lollipops, they throw themselves body and soul into entertaining the crowd. The audience cheers in delight. Taboo gives a joyful, energetic performance – a fantastic opening to the show!

"It was totally mad . . . but totally brilliant!"

Tina & Chandi

THROUGH TO THE FINAL

Connected

SEMI FINAL 3

"Step aside, there's a new kid on the block."

Philip Grimmer

It's this Madonna drag artist's birthday, and he intends to get the party started. Paul bursts onto the stage from a giant disco ball, wearing a sparkling purple leotard and knee-high boots. No one could call him shy! As he leans across Simon's desk, the audience is clapping along and cheering. But has he impressed the Judges?

Jimmy Forde

Guest judge Louis Walsh put this seventy-five-year-old leprechaun through at audition stage when Simon was off sick. Now it's up to Jimmy to convince Simon that Louis was right! He bounds onto the stage with a green beard, a pot of gold and a dancing human rainbow. Simon isn't convinced, but Louis is in the audience to defend his favourite!

"Authentic, fun, entertaining!"

The Arrangement

"You've got charisma."

The classical group with a twist are full of energy, eager to show the audience that they are capable of more than they did in their audition. Their fabulous front man, Jonathan, is buzzing with personality and enthusiasm. The audience goes wild!

SEMI FINAL 3

Chloe Hickinbottom

At the age of ten, Chloe is one of the youngest performers *Britain's Got Talent* has welcomed onto the stage. She loves singing, and it's all she wants to do! Chloe's wonderful audition performance means that she has a lot to live up to, and nerves are running high. But as she descends to the stage on a giant moon, her beautiful, mature voice soars out and entrances the Judges and the audience.

"I think you are destined for the West End."

Peridot

As Peridot's electrifying street-dancing skills ignite the stage, the audience cheers and applauds. Peridot are massively excited about this opportunity. They know that it could change everything for them! They have worked hard to achieve their dreams, and they know that now there is no room for error. There are lots of great dance groups this year – can they be the best?

"So far, by a mile, you are the best dance group."

Starburst

It's impossible not to smile when Starburst are performing! This happy, giggling dance troupe explodes onto the stage with a popular, upbeat routine. Simon says it's a million times better than their audition. The twenty-four performers open the show in bubbly, sensational style, and the Judges love them!

"I wish everybody would dance like you."

Christopher Stone

THROUGH TO THE FINAL

Paul Burling

SEMI FINAL 4

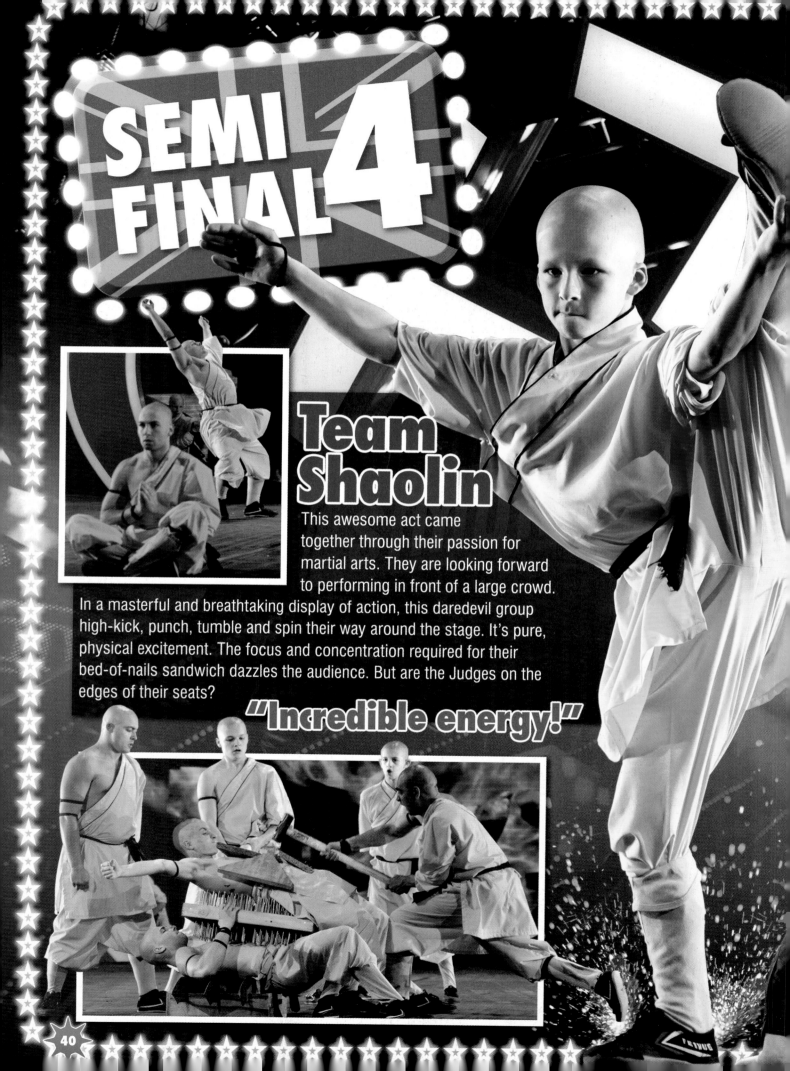

Team Shaolin

This awesome act came together through their passion for martial arts. They are looking forward to performing in front of a large crowd. In a masterful and breathtaking display of action, this daredevil group high-kick, punch, tumble and spin their way around the stage. It's pure, physical excitement. The focus and concentration required for their bed-of-nails sandwich dazzles the audience. But are the Judges on the edges of their seats?

"Incredible energy!"

Mark James

This ferry worker obviously loves every minute of performing onstage! His dual personality act belts out both parts of a famous duet, delighting the audience and entertaining Piers and Amanda enormously. Simon isn't so sure about getting two for the price of one, however!

"There's a lot of potential with this act."

Tyler Patterson

For Tyler, being in the semi-finals is better than Christmas! He knows that he has to make his moves bigger, faster and slicker, and prove that he deserves a place in the final. Dressed in an ultra-cool black and white suit, Tyler has the crowd going wild! His carefully planned routine comes entirely from his own imagination, and it's fresh, fun and entertaining. The Judges love it!

"You're a little dark horse."

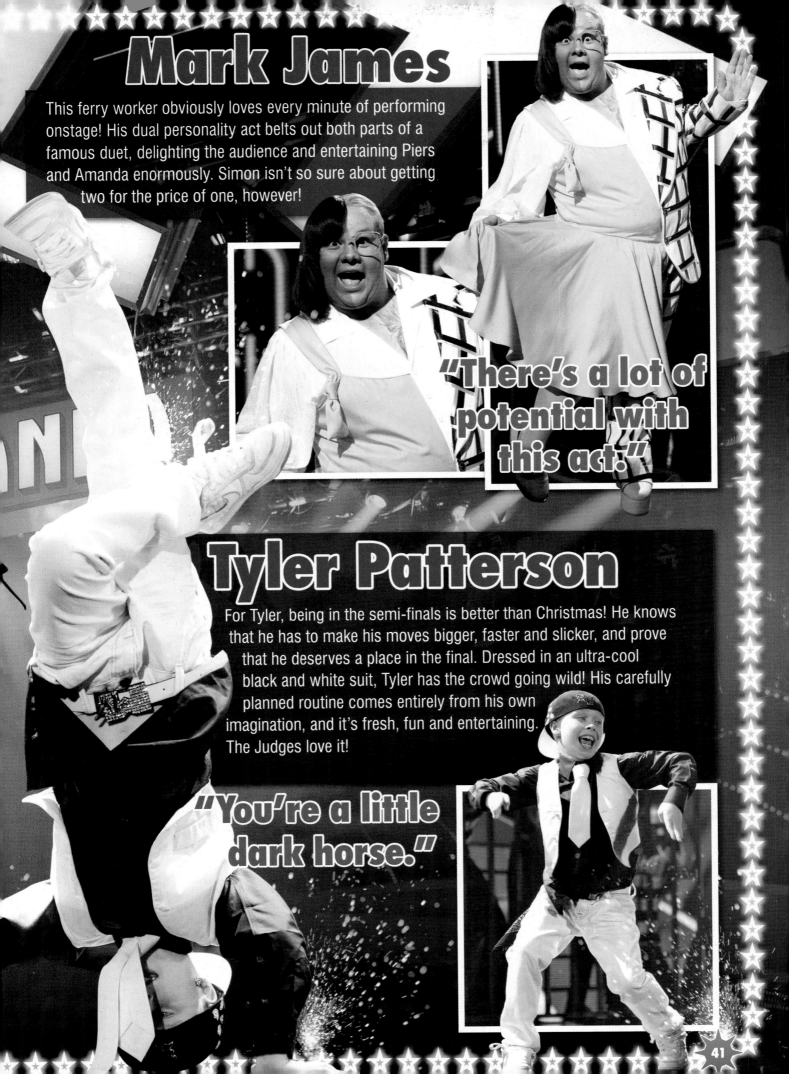

SEMI FINAL 4

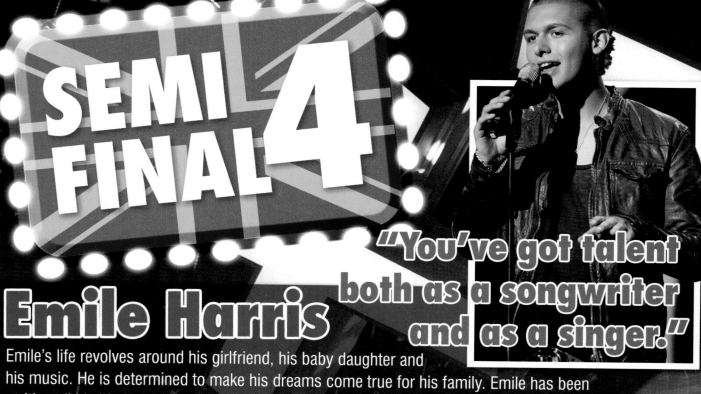

"You've got talent both as a songwriter and as a singer."

Emile Harris

Emile's life revolves around his girlfriend, his baby daughter and his music. He is determined to make his dreams come true for his family. Emile has been waiting all his life for this opportunity. But he takes a massive risk by performing a song that he has written himself. Dressed in casual clothes, Emile looks confident and relaxed, but unfortunately his gamble doesn't come off. Amanda and Piers press their buzzers halfway through the song, and all the Judges agreed that his audition was much better.

Ice

The first performers are Ice, hoping to keep cool under pressure! They give a seamless performance, incorporating throws, canes and Michael Jackson moves. But can their feisty attitude carry them to the final? Sadly, Amanda's positive comments aren't enough to soften the criticism from Simon and Piers.

"It was a little bit old-fashioned."

The Fusion

The audience and the Judges are thrilled by The Fusion's imaginative pirate-themed act. The dancers leap and bound around the stage in their skeletal costumes, filling the studio with electric energy. Even Simon, who buzzed them at audition stage, heaps praise on them tonight!

"The best act we've seen so far tonight."

Twist & Pulse

THROUGH TO THE FINAL

Janey Cutler

SEMI FINAL 5

"What you do is incredible."

Alesia Vazmitsel

Alesia sees pole dancing as an art form – can she persuade the audience to feel the same? She defies gravity, bringing the Judges and the audience to their feet. Her flexibility and strength are staggering. With perfect control, she makes her athletic performance seem easy. She performs at a great height without safety nets or harnesses, and she is still relaxed enough to smile!

Father & Son

Graham and James Edgington make all sorts of dreams come true just by standing onstage together. The Judges aren't convinced that their act is better than their audition, but Graham and James are just enjoying their chance to stand in the limelight!

"You sang well and you have a great relationship."

A3

These three brothers are overjoyed to have the chance to perform live onstage! They practise together at home and their family bond is incredibly strong. This chance could change their lives forever. They have worked hard to create a routine that will impress the Judges — and make their mum proud.

"You are actually very, very talented."

SEMI FINAL 5

Myztikal

"It was my favourite act of the night so far."

They only just got through their audition, so Myztikal are desperate to prove that they deserve to be here. Aged between ten and thirty, they developed their unique act by rehearsing in a supermarket car park!

The Chippendoubles

After The Chippendoubles' unforgettable audition performance, what can they do to convince the Judges that they have more to offer? They pour enthusiasm and fun into their act, but it's not enough to avoid buzzes from Simon and Piers.

"It was just you guys dancing around in silly shorts."

Dance Flavourz

Samba style explodes onto the *Britain's Got Talent* stage as Dance Flavourz makes a spectacular entrance. The act is a dizzying concoction of silver spangles, colourfully dressed beauties and music that makes everyone want to get up and dance – not to mention the giant silver elephant! The performance is a joyous, exuberant celebration that brings the Judges to their feet.

"You are just fabulous!"

Kieran Gaffney

THROUGH TO THE FINAL

Liam McNally

THE 2010

SIMON AMANDA PIERS

Thousands of hopefuls have auditioned, millions of viewers have voted, and it's all been leading up to one fantastic moment. It's here at last – the glittering final in which ten acts will be whittled down to just one.

The best of UK talent will share a stage, all hoping that this will be the night that all their dreams come true. A £100,000 cheque and a slot at the Royal Variety Performance awaits the winner.

The British public has voted, and the finalists have already come further than any of them dreamed possible. The taste of success is on their lips, but only one act will take the winner's title.

Tonight, the power is in the hands of the audience. Who is your winner?

The stage of dreams stands ready for the first act of the night, the Judges are brimming with excitement and the music is building to a crescendo.

THE *BRITAIN'S GOT TALENT* 2010 GRAND FINAL IS ABOUT TO BEGIN!

FINALISTS

TINA & CHANDI

PAUL BURLING

SPELBOUND

TWIST & PULSE

JANEY CUTLER

CONNECTED

CHRISTOPHER STONE

LIAM McNALLY

KIERAN GAFFNEY

TOBIAS MEAD

Liam McNally

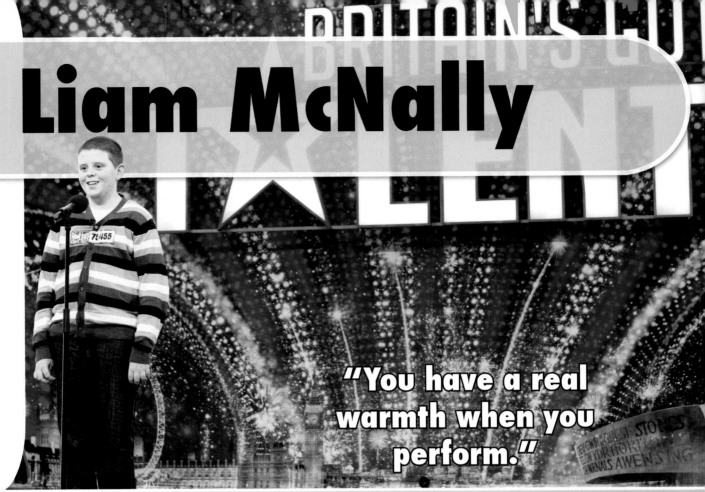

"You have a real warmth when you perform."

Fact File
Home town: New Moston, Manchester
Dream: To sing professionally
Job: Schoolboy
Talent: Singer

Fourteen-year-old Liam has loved singing for as long as he can remember. He wakes up and goes to sleep singing, so to appear on *Britain's Got Talent* really is a dream come true. His parents have no idea where his singing talent comes from, but they are determined to support him all the way. "I can't explain in words how proud I am," says his dad.

Audition

Liam's feeling hopeful and excited as he walks out onto the stage and prepares to perform to the biggest audience he's ever had.

As Liam sings the first few notes of *Danny Boy*, jaws drop all around the theatre. There is a burst of applause and then a hush falls – everyone wants to listen to Liam's wonderful voice. Liam smiles as he sings –

he's enjoying his performance immensely, and his warmth draws the audience to him. In the wings, his dad bites his lip and holds back tears of pride.

Judges' Reaction: The audience rises to its feet, whistling, cheering and applauding in delight. Liam gazes at them in wonder and happiness. The Judges can't wait to comment. "I wouldn't call you

a good singer," says Simon. "I would call you a fantastic singer." But he points out that at some point soon Liam's voice will break. "You have to enjoy and remember this moment," he adds.

"You are a serious contender to win *Britain's Got Talent*," says Piers. Amanda is bowled over by Liam's talent. "Your mum and dad must be so proud of you," she says.

Verdict: Liam sails through to the next stage of the competition.

Liam's Reaction: It will take a while for what just happened to sink in! But Liam is very happy.

Semi-Final

Liam stunned the Judges with his audition, and now he's under massive pressure to deliver a repeat performance. He's determined to enjoy his wonderful voice for as long as he can. Standing alone on the stage with only a microphone, Liam cuts a small figure – but what a voice!

A hush falls over the audience as the bell-like clarity of Liam's voice resounds around the studio. It's obvious that he's enjoying every moment. Piers rises to his feet and the audience erupts as the last notes die away.

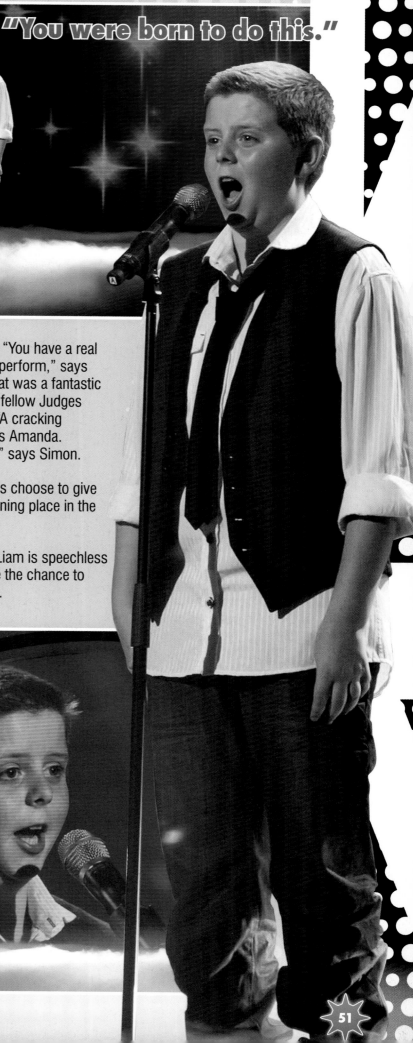

"You were born to do this."

Judges' Reaction: "You have a real warmth when you perform," says Piers. "I thought that was a fantastic performance." His fellow Judges agree completely. "A cracking performance," says Amanda. "Absolutely terrific," says Simon.

Verdict: The Judges choose to give Liam the last remaining place in the final.

Liam's Reaction: Liam is speechless with delight to have the chance to perform in the final.

"You have emotion."

51

"Tonight I'm going to go out and sing the best I've ever sung."

Final

In Liam's words: Backstage, Liam is on cloud nine just to be in the final of *Britain's Got Talent*. *"I need to grab this opportunity with both hands,"* he says. As the sound checks are performed, Liam prepares for the performance of a lifetime.

The lights go down and a single spotlight shines down on the young lad from Manchester. A pipe starts to play, and then Liam begins to sing the beautiful ballad that carried him through the audition. A breathless silence falls over the audience as they listen in wonder. When he reaches the crescendo, a chorus dressed all in white appears behind him, harmonising with his beautiful voice. It's a masterly performance.

"This is my last opportunity."

Judges' Reaction: "You've sung beautifully every time," says Piers. "You couldn't have done any more." Amanda agrees, adding, "You are such a credit to your

"When you sing you have fire in your eyes."

family… you're such a lovely young man." Simon's praise makes Liam's night complete.
"I loved you the first time we saw you," says Simon. "Tonight, astonishingly, you were note-perfect."

Liam's Reaction: Liam is very pleased with his performance – he knows that he has put the best of himself into it. It is just one day since he went through at the semi-final stage, so his feet have barely touched the ground!

"From the day I was born I was supposed to be a performer."

Janey Cutler

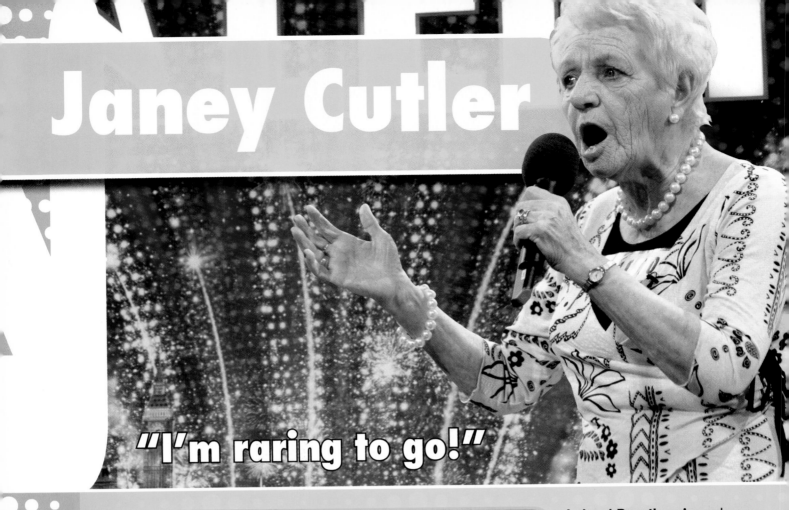

"I'm raring to go!"

Fact File

Home town: Wishaw, Scotland
Dream: To sing at the Royal Variety Performance
Job: Retired cleaner
Talent: Singer

At the age of eighty, Janey Cutler proves that you're never too old to meet a new challenge. She's a great-grandmother who walks her dog every day in her local park – and now she's taking on *Britain's Got Talent*! Her family is incredibly proud of her.

She first started singing when she was about six-years-old, as part of the Salvation Army. She grew up and had a family – life moved on, but her dream of singing onstage never left her.

Judges' Reaction: Amanda stands up to applaud; Piers joins her, grinning – even Simon is applauding! "You're so tiny and you have such a massive voice," says Amanda. "It was spectacular!"

Verdict: All the Judges agree that the Royal Family would love Janey, and she goes through to the semi-final.

Janey's Reaction: "*I didn't expect that, wait till I tell my friends!*" Janey exclaims as she comes off the stage.

Audition

Ant leads Janey onstage and she prepares to sing *No Regrets*. As her powerful voice soars out, she has the audience in the palm of her hand. People are on their feet – the applause is deafening, but Janey's voice rises above it all.

Her spirit and love of life are captured in the iconic song, and she looks completely at ease on stage. As she sings the last words, the whole theatre resounds with cheers, whistles and shouts. Janey looks up at the audience, breathless and delighted. This is a dream come true!

Semi-Final

Looking every inch the glamorous diva, Janey is escorted onto the stage by two handsome young men. In her red dress and pearls, she's the centre of attention.

As soon as she starts to sing, the audience is on its feet. The strength of her character lights up the stage, and it's clear that she's pouring everything she has into her performance.

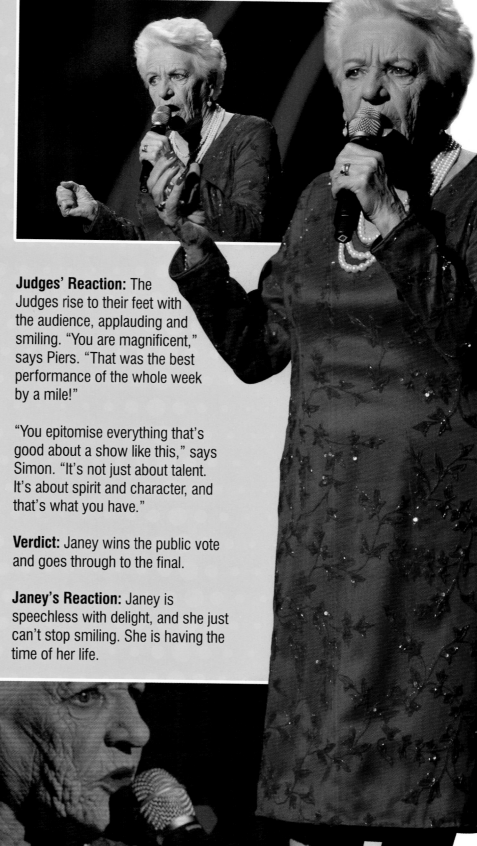

Judges' Reaction: The Judges rise to their feet with the audience, applauding and smiling. "You are magnificent," says Piers. "That was the best performance of the whole week by a mile!"

"You epitomise everything that's good about a show like this," says Simon. "It's not just about talent. It's about spirit and character, and that's what you have."

Verdict: Janey wins the public vote and goes through to the final.

Janey's Reaction: Janey is speechless with delight, and she just can't stop smiling. She is having the time of her life.

"She's the spirit of this competition."

Final

In Janey's words: *"I'm happy to be in the final, I didn't expect that to happen to me! Tonight I am going to sing my heart out."*

Dressed in elegant black with a red rose giving a riotous splash of colour, Janey looks magnificent onstage. She lifts her head and belts out her audition song *No Regrets*, backed by an orchestra. The smoke swirls around her ankles as she is illuminated by a starburst.

Although there is a tense moment when she seems to be out of sync with the live band, she recovers like a true professional and gets a rapturous reception from the audience.

"That was electrifying!"

Judges' Reaction: Piers praises Janey's ability to recover and perform, pointing out that this is live TV and anything can happen. "You are a remarkable lady," he says, "that was a great performance and a great recovery."

"The last part of that song was terrific," says Amanda. Simon agrees, saying how impressed he is that she was able to get back in time and give a spectacular performance. "You are one gutsy lady," he tells her.

"I am here to win."

Janey's Reaction:

"Well I hope it was all right," says Janey with her irrepressible smile. Whatever the outcome of the final, Janey has achieved something that she has been dreaming of since she was a little girl.

One thing's for sure; Janey's magnificent voice will continue to entertain audiences throughout Glasgow, and no one will ever forget this fabulous finalist.

"I'm going to remember this performance for a very long time."

Christopher Stone

"That was probably the scariest thing I've ever done in my life"

Fact File

Home town: North Rigton, Yorkshire
Dream: To sing professionally
Job: Accountant
Talent: Singer

Until now, Christopher Stone has always lacked the courage to reach for the stars. He works as an accountant and admits that his day-to-day life can be boring. His job pays the bills, but it is his heartfelt dream to be a singer. With the support of his parents, he has finally seized his opportunity. Can he make his dream a reality?

Audition

Christopher's parents are here to support him on his big day. It's thanks to them that he has come along to audition.

They know how much singing means to him, and they long for him to realise his dream. Christopher is petrified, but as he walks out onstage he knows that he has to conquer his nerves and seize this opportunity with both hands.

Despite his fears, his voice rings out clear and true. People sit enraptured, their hands cupped around their faces. When the song ends, the audience responds with delighted cheers and applause.

Judges' Reaction: "I would say the issue with you is your lack of conviction," says Simon, noticing how Christopher is wringing his hands. "I don't feel an awful lot of self-belief about you." However, he adds that Christopher has a really good voice. "It was brilliant, I loved your voice," says Amanda. Piers agrees, hoping Christopher will start to believe in himself.

Verdict: It's unanimous – the Judges want to see Christopher in the semi-finals!

Christopher's Reaction: *"That was probably the scariest thing I've ever done in my life, I felt about twenty feet high!"* His performance has changed everything and his dream is looking closer than ever before.

Semi-Final

Tonight could change Christopher's life forever. Now he has to believe in himself and show the Judges what he's made of. Choosing a song that embodies everything he stands for, Christopher sings *The Impossible Dream*. As smoke swirls around him and a backdrop of stars twinkles, he gives the performance of a lifetime. He uses the nerves and focuses them on the performance, channelling all his energies into the song.

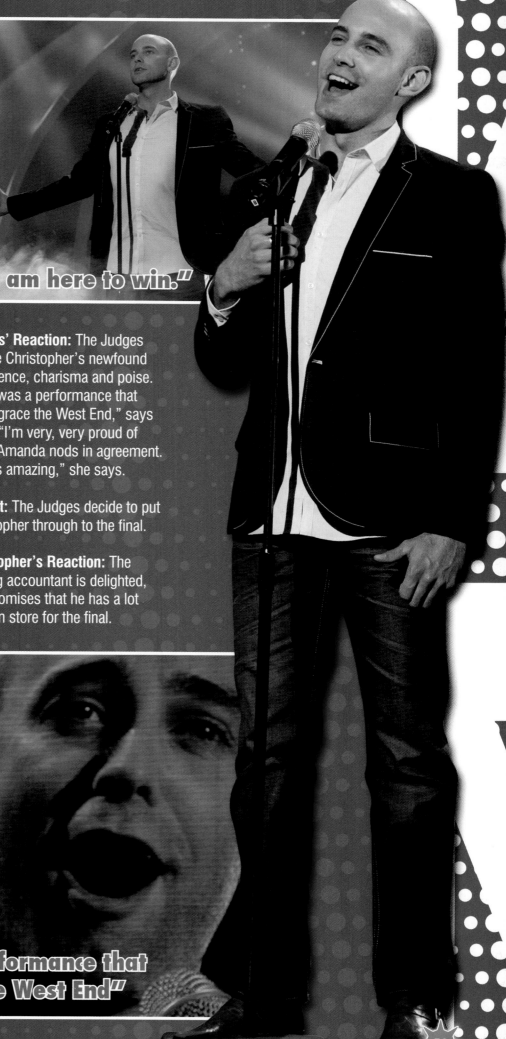

"I am here to win."

Judges' Reaction: The Judges admire Christopher's newfound confidence, charisma and poise. "That was a performance that could grace the West End," says Piers. "I'm very, very proud of you." Amanda nods in agreement. "It was amazing," she says.

Verdict: The Judges decide to put Christopher through to the final.

Christopher's Reaction: The singing accountant is delighted, and promises that he has a lot more in store for the final.

"That was a performance that could grace the West End"

"One day I might not need a calculator any more
– someone else can do my tax return!"

Final

In Christopher's words: *"It is an amazing feeling to be told that you're getting through to the final. To win this competition would completely change my life."* he explains.

Christopher strides onstage, looking every inch the performer. This really is his chance to live the dream...

Being in the final is the biggest opportunity he has ever had – will he make the most of it? He sings with simplicity and soulful feeling, pouring emotion and truth into the words with a conviction that has the audience spellbound. His eyes are sparkling with confidence and self-belief. He looks as if he has been performing all his life – the transformation from the shy man who auditioned is absolute.

SIMON   AMANDA   PIERS

"You were born to do this."

"I'm not just som
boring accountant

60

Judges' Reaction: Piers is blown away by the performance and encourages Christopher to give up his job as an accountant and get onto the West End stage. "You're unrecognisable from the shy, nerve-wracked guy we saw in the audition," he says. Amanda comments on the heart and longing that she saw in Christopher's performance, and tells him how moved she was by it. "You are a naturally gifted, great singer," says Simon, agreeing with his fellow Judges.

"He's terrific."

Christopher's Reaction: *"That was just fantastic – the most wonderful feeling ever, I felt so comfortable and so happy!"*

Christopher's personal journey to overcome his nerves has brought him here, and he has achieved something that he has been dreaming of all his life. Whatever the results of the final, he can hold his head high, for his future surely holds great things.

"From the day I was born I was supposed to be a performer."

Paul Burling

"It's a variety competition and I think it needs comedy in the final

Audition

Paul walks onstage knowing that this is the big opportunity he has been waiting for. He's waited twenty years to be seen on TV, and the moment has finally arrived. He's determined not to mess it up.

Paul delivers a laugh-a-minute quick-fire routine that has the audience and the Judges laughing along with him. From Harry Hill to Scooby Doo, he races through a cast of well-loved characters that are instantly recognisable. By the end of the performance the audience is on its feet – they love Paul's act, but what do the Judges think?

Judges' Reaction: The Judges are smiling, and that's a good sign! "You are the best impressionist we've ever seen," says Piers. Amanda is thrilled to think that *Britain's Got Talent* has discovered a new star. "It was just incredible to see how much it meant to you when you got the reaction you got from the audience."

Verdict: The Judges agree that Paul deserves to go through to the semi-finals.

Paul's Reaction: Paul struggles to put his overpowering emotions into words. *"It means so much, I've got children who I adore and they adore me… I want them to be proud of their dad."*

Semi-Final

Paul's act begins with a repeat of his uncanny impression of Harry Hill. He races through a gallery of famous characters including comedy acts, soap stars and film stars. His comic timing, gags and innovation keep everyone laughing, and even Simon's grinning. Will *Britain's Got Talent* enable him to make his dreams of stardom come true?

Judges' Reaction: "If you don't make the final it will be a total travesty," says Piers, who has really enjoyed Paul's jokes.

"You are the best impressionist we've had." Amanda and Simon agree that they want to see him in the final.

Verdict: Paul wins the public vote, as the studio audience cheer.

Paul's Reaction: When Paul hears that he has won the audience vote, he can hardly believe his ears! He clutches his head in disbelief. *"I'm still in a little bit of shock!"* he says. After all this time, is his dream finally going to come true?

"You're a natural entertainer."

"You've worked twenty-five years for this opportunity."

Final

In Paul's words: Paul knows that it's time to spread his wings and see how far he can fly. *"I've been doing the holiday parks thing for years now, Britain's Got Talent's given me a whole new lease of life."* He's just one step away from the Royal Variety performance. Tonight he's going to do everything he can to win the contest.

Paul's musical impressions act has the audience clapping along from the start.
Using voices from TV shows, comedy sketches and cartoons he soon has the audience squealing and whistling in delight. The variety of voices is dizzying and his skill in switching between them all at speed is magnificent. Although Paul makes it look easy, singing a chorus using

"Worthy of a Royal Variety place."

thirteen different voices is a feat of control, concentration and determination that not many could achieve.

Judges' Reaction: As the audience claps, stamps its feet and laughs, the Judges are smiling. "I loved it!" Piers exclaims. "You came up with an inspired routine." His fellow Judges are just as delighted with Paul's musical comedy turn.

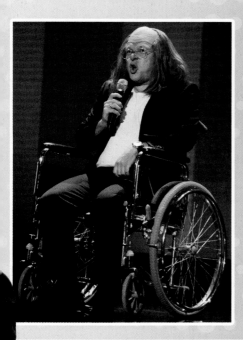

"You're a big bag of comedy voices!" Amanda says with a laugh. Simon agrees, adding, "I think it was really, really funny and inventive".

Paul's Reaction: When asked how he feels, Paul has just two words:

"Absolutely amazing!" The chance to display his talent on national TV has invigorated him, and he is fizzing with energy and hope for the future. Thanks to *Britain's Got Talent*, great things lie ahead for Paul!

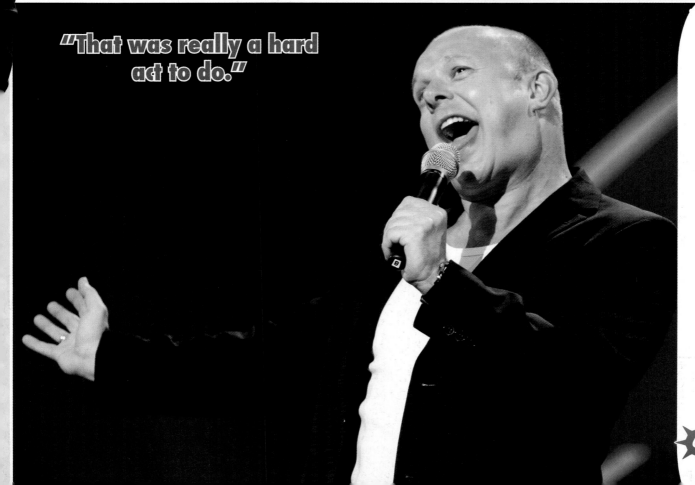

"That was really a hard act to do."

Connected

"I got goose pimples the minute you all started singing"

Fact File

Home town: Manchester, Lancashire
Dream: Touring & contracts
Job: Schoolboys
Talent: Singers

Young boy band Connected hope that they are the future of pop music. Connor, Harry, Matt, Max and Miles are the best of friends. They're thrilled to have the chance to perform and can't wait to get out onstage and show what they can do. Their mums helped to put the group together, and are here to support them all the way.

Audition

From the moment the boys walk onto the stage, it's obvious that they are enjoying every minute. As soon as they start singing, their harmonies and moves have the audience on their feet, and an air of excitement sweeps through the audience. Is this a glimpse of the future of pop music?

Simon isn't sure – he wants to know if they can create an original look and sound. Eagerly, Connected perform another song to try to convince Simon. It's a huge hit with the audience, and the boys' eyes are alight with hope as they gaze at the cheering crowd. This is their first taste of fame, and they love it!

Judges' Reaction: "I got goose pimples the minute you all started singing," says Amanda. "You've got a very big future ahead of you." Piers agrees, but Simon is still concerned that the group isn't original enough. However, he singles out Harry for particular praise, and agrees that they need some professional support.

Verdict: The boys go straight through to the semi-finals.

Connected's Reaction: The boys feel incredible when they come offstage. *"The most amazing experience,"* they agree. Their mums are equally as excited!

Semi-Final

The question on everybody's lips is whether Connected are going to rise to the challenge Simon has set them. He's hoping to see a more modern routine, so the boys have taken control of their look, their harmonies and their choreography. Will it pay off?

The five boys walk onstage and start to sing. Their song builds into a crescendo of emotion and harmony. It's an uplifting song that focuses on the bond between them and forges a powerful connection to the audience.

"Absolutely knockout"

Judges' Reaction: The Judges are all impressed. "Absolutely knockout," Piers says with a smile. "You are showing us the future this evening," Amanda adds. Simon's praise is the sweetest of all to the boys. "You've got a real shot now," he says.

Verdict: The Judges vote Connected through to the final.

Connected's Reaction: The boys are overwhelmed to be through to the final!

"You've got a real shot now"

67

"We practise all the time every day."

Final

In Connected's words: *"Being in the final feels absolutely amazing, It's more than a dream come true for us."* To succeed tonight they have to be note-perfect and do every move right. Can they give the performance of their lives?

Standing in a line onstage, the boys look comfortable and relaxed – and totally ready for all the fame that life can throw at them! They sing with energy, joy and passion, smiling as the audience cheers and claps along in time with the music. But is it enough to carry them to the Royal Variety Performance?

SIMON AMANDA PIERS

"We're all in this together."

"We get our kicks out of singing."

68

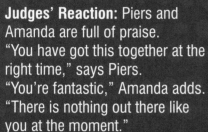

Judges' Reaction: Piers and Amanda are full of praise. "You have got this together at the right time," says Piers. "You're fantastic," Amanda adds. "There is nothing out there like you at the moment."

However, Simon is disappointed. He thinks that their song choice stopped them being unique. "I like you guys and I think you've got great potential," he says. "But I think you could have done something that made you different from everyone else."

Connected's Reaction: Rocked by the highs and lows of the evening, the boys stand close together as applause ricochets around the studio. Each of them put their heart and soul into the act, and no one can ask for more. Delighted by all the support they've had, they can hardly believe it when they hear that their idols JLS are supporting them.

Whatever happens when the results come in, the boys agree that this has been an unforgettable, life-changing experience!

"These kids are determined and focused."

"That was just the best experience of my life!"

Tina and Chandi

"Chandi is an amazingly talented performer."

Fact File

Home town: Shrewsbury, Shropshire
Dream: To show the UK what Chandi can do
Job: Music teacher and man's best friend
Talent: Dancing dog

Tina and Chandi are best friends and soulmates. Tina rescued Chandi from a dog pound when she was four-months-old. They have been inseparable ever since. "I think it was fate," says Tina. Chandi is now nearly twelve-years-old, and Tina is determined to show everybody how beautiful and talented her little rescue dog is.

Piers feels sorry that Simon has missed seeing this act through sickness. He'd have loved it! But luckily replacement Judge Louis Walsh is just as pleased. "The best dog act I've ever seen," says Louis in delight. "I think Chandi is a star."

Verdict: Tina and Chandi have no trouble getting through to the semi-finals!

Tina and Chandi's Reaction: Tina and Chandi are delighted to have the chance to perform again.

Audition

Tina and Chandi walk confidently onstage, ready to show the Judges and the audience what hard work and love can achieve. As the music starts, the audience gasps in astonishment. Chandi is doing ballet! The crowd oohs and ahhs in delight. Chandi is incredibly agile and clearly loves every moment. When Chandi gives a doggy bow, there is no doubt that she has won every heart in the theatre.

Judges' Reaction: The Judges are delighted with Chandi and heap praise on her and Tina. "It's just so lovely to see your relationship," says Amanda. "She really wants to please you – to thank you for looking after her, I think."

Semi-Final

Dressed in coordinating hot pink outfits, Tina and Chandi perform a routine that's packed with warmth, humour and friendship. The audience laughs, cheers and claps as Chandi performs like a professional, gazing up adoringly at Tina.

The applause is thunderous and no one seems to want to stop. Tina is clearly delighted at the reception her best friend is getting, but Chandi is only interested in Tina's reaction.

Judges' Reaction: Simon has never seen Chandi perform live and the audience is on tenterhooks to know what he thinks. "I love her," says Simon. "It just shows you how important it is to love a dog, because that dog will love you back."

Amanda's heart has been touched. "I can feel myself welling up just because of the affection I can see between you," she says.

Verdict: Tina and Chandi win the audience vote and head for the final.

Tina's's Reaction: Tina can't believe that they have the chance to perform in the final!

"Being in the semi-finals with my best friend is absolutely amazing."

71

"This is Chandi's moment to shine."

Final

In Tina's words: *"Chandi is the centre of my world, I just absolutely adore her."* Tina has never forgotten the tough start that Chandi had in a dog's home, and she feels that it would be a phenomenal achievement for Chandi to perform at the Royal Variety Performance. She knows that the risks and pressure on them both are immense, but if Chandi can handle it, then so can she!

Dressed in a gleaming white tail suit (and patriotic socks!), Tina looks every inch the Hollywood diva, and Chandi's matching neckscarf makes her look like a star. With a glittering New York backdrop and music from the golden days of swing, the audience is in for something special.

Their routine is fun, seemingly effortless and inspired, and it's easy to see that Chandi loves every minute.

"We do everything together."

72

The atmosphere in the studio is warm, and all hearts are touched by this incredible partnership. It's fun, unexpected and moving, and the audience loves it.

Judges' Reaction: The Judges are as impressed as the audience. "I think it's such a charming act that you do," says Piers. "Chandi's a wonderfully intelligent and sensitive dog, and looks so happy. You've got such a special chemistry – it's a lovely act to watch."

"I think it was another fantastic routine," says Amanda. "Chandi's just adorable. The bond between you is amazing." Simon is just as enthusiastic. "She's a very special dog," he says.

Tina's Reaction: Chandi's wagging tail says it all – she loved every moment of her performance!

"I'm just her sidekick!" Tina says with a happy laugh.

"Woof!"

"I am so pleased with her!"

73

Tobias Mead

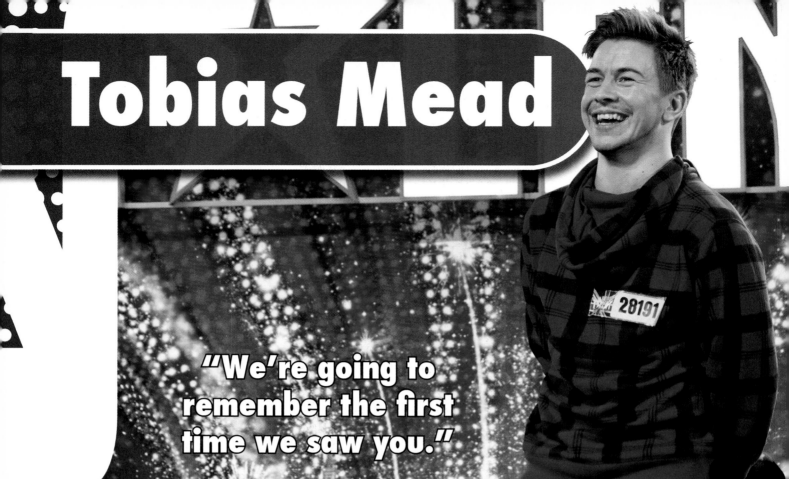

"We're going to remember the first time we saw you."

Fact File
Home town: London / Wiltshire
Dream: To entertain
Job: Dancer
Talent: Dancer

Tobias Mead's dad wanted him to be a footballer, but all Tobias wants to do is dance. When he was younger he played football for his county and had a lot of potential, but his heart wasn't in it. He's taking this opportunity to reach for his dream. At the age of twenty-two, has his big chance finally arrived?

Audition

The music starts and Tobias starts to dance. **He obviously has talent – his movements are easy and fluid.** The audience cheers – and then squeals in astonishment and excitement. Tobias has turned around to reveal a mask on the back of his head. With a hood pulled over his face the effect is surreal and disturbing! No one can take their eyes off him as he performs his totally unique and hugely surprising routine.

Judges' Reaction: The audience rises to its feet – Ant and Dec are applauding in the wings. Tobias's performance has sent everyone wild! "I honestly was blown away by that," Amanda says. "It was like your body was made out of liquid." But the audience boos Piers when he suggests that Tobias should have covered more ground.

Simon has the last word. "I'm going to agree with Amanda," he says. "Every so often somebody comes along who is just brilliant."

Verdict: Three resounding yesses send Tobias through to the semi-finals!

Tobias's Reaction: *"Wow, I was not expecting that from Simon!"* says Tobias.

Semi-Final

Since finding out that he was through to the semi-finals, Tobias has poured all his time and energy into creating a routine that will really make the Judges sit up and take notice. "I'm going to be doing something that's never been done on British TV before," he says.

Searchlights illuminate the stage and the sound of police sirens and helicopters fills the air. The tension rises as the audience looks for Tobias. Then he springs from backstage high into the air! A silver sphere floats beside him as he body pops across the stage. It's a dazzling fusion of street dance and street magic. He ends with a cheeky wink timed perfectly with the music.

"I felt like Michael Jackson for a minute."

Judges' Reaction: The Judges are delighted with Tobias's performance, and all three agree that he has created something innovative, clever and impressive.

Verdict: The Judges choose to put Tobias through the final.

Tobias's Reaction: *"Being in the semi-final is the highlight of my life, I feel over the moon!"* Tobias beams.

"I want to be the person that comes out on top."

Final

In Tobias's words: *"I'm absolutely ecstatic to be in the final,"* he says. Don't be fooled by the twinkle in his eye – Tobias has been having the time of his life and he's here to win!

Tobias knows that he has to make tonight's performance more meticulous, creative and challenging than anything he has done before. This has to be the best performance ever.

In a scene straight from the pages of Dracula, the stage is thick with mist and two coffins stand upright onstage. Eerie music echoes around the studio. The audience are breathless with anticipation. Hanging upside down like a bat, Tobias drops from the ceiling and, with a crack of lightning, the routine begins.

"You only live once!"

"I got masses of goose bumps then."

As dancers writhe on the stage and howls fill the air, Tobias puts on a performance that fuses all the best moments from his previous routines and adds plenty of new ones into the bargain. His incredible fluid movements and inventive moves stun and delight the audience. This is something that *Britain's Got Talent* has never seen before.

Judges' Reaction: Piers praises Tobias for putting on a show and says that he is the best dancer in the competition. Amanda agrees, adding, "your creativity and imagination is second to none."

"You are really, really super-talented."

"That was incredible."

"You did everything you should have done on the biggest night of your life," affirms Simon. "You turned it up a notch, you made it very current."

Tobias's Reaction: Tobias is ecstatic with the response.

"Thank you so much for this opportunity to be here, If it wasn't for this show, I wouldn't be able to do what's going on in my head." he says.

"That was the best thing I've ever done."

Kieran Gaffney

3rd Place

Fact File

Home town: Kent
Dream: To drum professionally
Job: Schoolboy
Talent: Drummer

Kieran Gaffney's dream has been on hold for a year, but his focus has never faded or wavered. Drumming is a passion for this schoolboy – he's crammed with potential and determination. He hopes to show everyone that drumming can be exciting, creative and entertaining. Can he and his drum kit impress the audience and the Judges? Can Kieran's dream come true?

Audition

Last year, Kieran did well in his audition but didn't make it through to the semi-finals. This year he's determined to come back better, stronger and louder than ever!

At first, however, it all seems to be going wrong. He auditions with his parents, and the Judges aren't keen on their performance. Kieran is thrilled to be given another chance to audition – this time on his own. With no time to prepare, he has to improvise a solo on the spot. He throws himself into his performance, but is it enough to please the Judges?

Judges' Reaction: The audience goes crazy – they love it! They clap along as the infectious beat fills the theatre. When the performance ends, the audience rises to its feet.

"Oh Kieran, I'm so proud of you," says Amanda. "You played for your life then!" Piers agrees, adding, "You are an incredibly talented drummer." Simon is just as impressed as his fellow Judges.

Verdict: Kieran gets three yesses from the Judges and is put through to the semi-finals.

Kieran's Reaction: Kieran comes off the stage to a proud hug from his dad. His dream is still burning brightly. *"I feel great, I wanted to do it for my mum and dad as well."*

"For a drummer to do that to an audience – amazing!"

"It just goes to show that you should never give up on your goal."

"I love drumming –
it means the world to me."

Semi-Final

Flashing lights illuminate the stage as Kieran channels all his love of drumming, all his passion and energy into his performance.

Kieran has waited a long time for this moment. It's almost possible to see the beat travelling through him! His drumsticks have become an extension of his body, and with one last electrifying crash of drums, the performance is over. Audience and Judges are on their feet, whooping and cheering.

"This year could be his year."

Judges' Reaction: "You are a little fighter . . . I absolutely loved it," says Piers. Amanda agrees, feeling overjoyed for the boy. "An absolutely stunningly brilliant performance," adds Simon.

Verdict: Kieran wins the popular audience vote.

Kieran's Reaction: Kieran buries his face in his hands for a moment, trying to take it in. Then he looks up, a beaming smile lighting up his face. *"I feel over the moon, Thank you very much, everyone!"*

"I'm going to go for this with all my heart, passion and soul."

Final

In Kieran's words: Kieran has been swamped by almost overwhelming emotions of joy and disbelief. *"Last night when they called my name… I cried a bit,"* he says with a wry smile.

"Tonight there are no second chances; I need to get it right."

On a platform that floats high above the stage, Kieran sits like a King of Drums, setting the whole studio on fire with his performance.

"Those drums were on fire tonight!"

The platform tilts from side to side like a flying saucer and the audience erupts into a cacophony of whistles, screams and cheers.

Judges' Reaction: The Judges cannot praise Kieran enough. The fact that he came back after having been rejected the year before shows guts and determination – and embodies the spirit of *Britain's Got Talent.*

"You are a showman," says Simon, impressed by the fact that it was Kieran's idea to drum on a floating platform. "You've got real passion and enthusiasm."

Kieran's Reaction: Kieran feels amazing and has loved every minute of his performance on this night of nights. Learning that the viewers have voted him one of the top three variety acts in the whole of the UK is the icing on the cake.

The whirlwind of praise and support that has brought Kieran here lifts his confidence and his happiness to the rafters – nothing can change that! *"Thank you very much, thank you everyone for supporting me. Thank you!"* Kieran Gaffney, a true gentleman – and an amazing drummer!

3RD BRITAIN'S GOT TALENT PLACE

83

Twist and Pulse

Runners up – 2nd Place

"Everything we do onstage is what we're like as people."

Fact File

Home town: Catford / Belvedere, London
Dream: To be professional dancers
Job: Students
Talent: Street dance

Ashley and Glen are best friends who share a love of street dance and a fantastic sense of humour. They rehearse as much as they can at each other's houses – getting under their parents' feet! Their dream is to use their original talent to make their dreams come true. Their determination and self-belief is inspiring, and underneath their laid-back humour is a focus that they hope will take them all the way to the final.

Judges' Reaction: The audience gives the boys a standing ovation – they enjoyed every minute of the inventive, unusual routine. "I thought that was terrific," says Piers. "That was one of the most exciting, original routines we've seen!" Amanda agrees. "You danced to every section of the music and you told a story," she says. Simon is also impressed. "I thought the routine was incredibly well worked out," he says.

Audition

When Twist and Pulse walk **onstage, no one knows what to expect.** But as soon as the music starts and their inventive, funny and clever dance routine begins, the audience goes wild! They have never seen anything like it – but they love it. The comic timing and the connection between Ashley and Glen make for a routine that's full of skill and laughter.

Verdict: The Judges choose to put Ashley and Glen through to the semi-finals. The boys are speechless with delight. They've already come a long way from practising in the kitchen, and now they are one step closer to making their dreams come true. Their ambition has become a reality, and now the sky's the limit!

Twist and Pulse's Reaction: The boys are so excited by the Judges' reactions that they can't stop smiling! But this is where the hard work really has to start.

Twist and Pulse hurry away from the auditions, eager to start planning a new routine at once. The more time they have to prepare and rehearse, the better their act will become.

And they are determined to prove to the Judges and the audience that they deserve a place in the final…

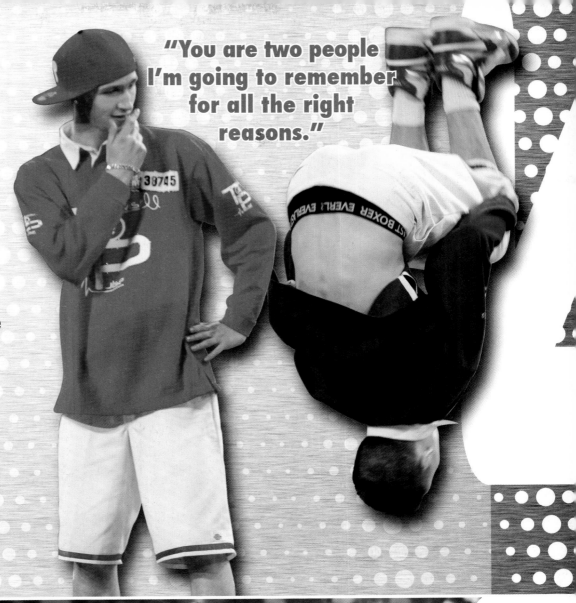

"You are two people I'm going to remember for all the right reasons."

"Twist and Pulse are going to go for it!"

"We need to make sure that we can raise the game."

Semi-Final

However nervous Twist and Pulse might feel, they look cool when they step onto the stage. They dance and joke their way through a performance that's full of energy, fun and enthusiasm, and yet they make it look easy!

The boys have a humorous, friendly and modern attitude that shines through their routine. Their engaging personalities, coupled with their determination and sense of fun, create an unforgettable act. The audience is engaged and delighted, and people are jumping to their feet to applaud. It's an intricate, intelligent performance with an impeccable sense of comedy.

When the routine comes to an end, the boys give their characteristic cheeky grins and the audience rises to its feet. The cheers, whistles and shouts are deafening – Ant and Dec can't get a word in!

Judges' Reaction: The Judges appreciate the fact that they are seeing something new. "It's just genius," says Amanda. "The moves are so intricate." Piers feels that the boys have been the best dance act in the competition. "Everything about that came from you," Simon adds. "It's unique."

Verdict: The Judges decide to put Twist and Pulse through to the final, with Amanda getting the casting vote. It's a tough decision to have to make, as all the acts have put their heart and soul into their routines. But it's obvious that Twist and Pulse are hugely popular, and the audience is thrilled when they are given the opportunity to go to the next stage of the competition.

Twist and Pulse's Reaction: *"We've been working so hard,"* they say happily. Their hearts are hammering with excitement. Ashley started dancing six years ago and Glen started five years ago. The thought that all their hard work and determination is paying off is hugely rewarding.

In the two years since they met, they have developed a bond that adds magic to their performances.

"You just showed us a glimpse of the future."

"It is the best of the best now."

Final

In Twist and Pulse's words: Twist and Pulse can hardly believe that they are in the final. They came along to the auditions with something new and original, and that is what *Britain's Got Talent* is really all about.

"Doing this together as best friends makes it so much better, we have the same sense of humour and we find each other funny."

The lads descend to the stage on poles and the streetcomedy begins! So much happens that, as the audience is applauding one move, another has them laughing or gasping.

Combining eye-popping dance moves with warm humour, the boys create an unforgettable routine. The audience responds with enthusiasm – this is one of the most popular acts of the night.

Judges' Reaction: The Judges are delighted with the boys' routine. "You have set the bar tonight," says Piers. "It was fantastic." Amanda tells the boys how much she has enjoyed watching them. "I love you," she says. "You're on the money!" But the biggest praise comes from Simon. "For me this was the best routine we've seen from you so far," he states. "You're incredibly current… I'm really impressed."

Twist and Pulse's Reaction: Twist and Pulse are delighted with the Judges' comments and agree that the feeling onstage has been incredible. They learn that they are runners up in the biggest variety show in the country – this is an incredible achievement!

"Winning tonight could change a lot for us."

2ND
BRITAIN'S GOT T★LENT PLACE

Spelbound
Winners

> "We spent years dedicating our lives to our gymnastics training."

Fact File

Home town: Ashford, Middlesex

Dream: To win *Britain's Got Talent*

Talent: Gymnastics

Gymnasts: 13 members, Amy Mackenzie 12, Hollianne Wood 13, Abigail Ralph 15, Jonathan Stranks 15, Lauren Kemp 17, Katie Axten 17, Leighanne Cowler 18, Edward Upcott 18, Douglas Fordyce 19, Adam McAssey 20, Adam Buckingham 21, Alex Uttley 24, Nicholas Illingworth 24.

Spelbound is an acrobatic gymnastic troupe of best friends ranging between the ages of twelve and twenty-four. They've watched *Britain's Got Talent* for years, and have dreamed of performing on that glittering stage. They're all from different backgrounds, but their shared love of gymnastics has brought them together.

Audition

As the Judges wish Spelbound luck and the music starts, no one has any idea of the spectacle they are about to see. The troupe's coach, Neil, has put together a routine that makes jaws hit the floor. Bodies spin through the air; there are human skipping ropes and tumbling backflips. In the wings, Ant and Dec can hardly believe what is happening in front of their eyes.

Judges' Reaction: People in the audience point and gasp in wonder and disbelief. Simon's eyes open wide in amazement. "I have never seen anything like that in my life," he says, genuinely bowled over. "I thought that once again we were going to get some really boring gymnastics display but that was very clever – really, really smart."

> "These kids are determined and focused."

Amanda is on her feet. "It was absolutely faultless," she enthuses. "Some of the stuff that was going on I didn't think was humanly possible. Absolutely incredible."

Piers agrees that it has been a thrilling performance. "You had the whole theatre going crazy," he tells the delighted gymnasts.

Verdict: The audience cheers and applauds – they have just seen something that they will never forget. People were literally holding their breath as the gymnasts whirled above the stage. The Judges have no hesitation in putting Spelbound through to the next stage.

Spelbound's Reaction:

In the wings, Neil is beaming with pride. The gymnasts leap up and down and hug each other – all their hard work has paid off! Most of the members of the troupe have been training since the age of four, so this is a massive boost to their confidence and their hopes.

However, the elation they feel must now be channelled into creating an even better routine. For the semi-final, they must dazzle the audience on a totally new level. Each of the performers must be dedicated to achieving perfection.

They are all willing to do whatever it takes to win a place in the final. That means getting up early every day to train and then meeting again after school and work to train some more.

In the run-up to the semi-final, Spelbound will eat, sleep and breathe *Britain's Got Talent*. These gymnasts have amazing powers of concentration and focus. Now they must use those strengths to create an even more exciting and captivating routine.

Semi-Final

Spelbound were so good the first time around – what can they possibly do to improve? The audience soon gets an answer to that question! Flames erupt onstage as the flying gymnasts spring into action.

With a theme of fire and ice, the whirling gymnasts really seem to have the gift of flight. Without safety nets or ropes they spin and twirl high above the stage. There's so much going on that it's hard to know where to look!

Judges' Reaction: "That was one of the most extraordinary routines," Piers gasps. Amanda agrees, adding that Spelbound would be fantastic ambassadors for Great Britain. Simon is equally impressed. "I've never seen anything in this country as good as this," he says. "Absolutely superb!"

"We've worked so hard for this – we don't want to go home."

"We just love to perform."

"Outstanding!"

Verdict: The audience puts Spelbound through to the final and one step closer to the Royal Variety Performance.

Spelbound's Reaction: Neil has to hold back tears of pride. *"It's an absolutely amazing feeling, to go on and get to the final is just a dream come true for us."*

"One of the most astonishing things I have ever seen."

Final

In Spelbound's words: The troupe has spent years learning to perform as one. For the final, they want to get the moves higher, harder and even more exciting. Above all, they want to go out onstage and entertain, proving what they do is worthy of the Royal Variety Performance.

Spelbound's performance begins with a death-defying flight across the Judges' desk. There are many incredible feats of balance and strength to watch, but the beautiful symmetry of the performance makes it work as one routine. Gymnasts balance on the heads of other performers using only one hand, human towers stand three people high, and the troupe members swing, roll and spin through the air. The entire audience erupts into cheers and applause.

Judges' Reaction: Piers says that he believes Spelbound truly represents the best of Britain's talent. Amanda can hardly find words strong enough to praise them. "You're so professional and so slick and disciplined," she says, going on to say that Spelbound should be the opening act for the 2012 Olympics. Simon agrees. "Putting it into Olympic terms," he says, "that would have won the gold medal."

Spelbound's Reaction: The gymnasts are delighted with how their routine went. They have rehearsed over and over again and this performance went absolutely to plan. But despite the audience reaction and the Judges' praise, it all depends on the viewers at home.

When Ant and Dec announce that Spelbound have won, the troupe is filled with joy, happiness and shock. Their dreams really have come true!

"Amanda, thank you for letting me fly over your head!"

"There's a lot more risk in tonight's routine."

Popular Winners:
Since winning *Britain's Got Talent*, Spelbound have been very busy! They could never have imagined how dramatically they would be catapulted into the limelight. They chose to enter the competition to promote gymnastics, with no idea of what the future might hold for them.

The gymnasts had many interviews with TV, radio, newspapers and magazines, before heading back to the gym to carry on training. Suddenly, in addition to preparing for the World Championships, they have an array of exciting new offers to consider.

"High-voltage excellence."

New Opportunities:
Usher was at the final and has said that he would like to work with the troupe, and internet clips of their performances have already made them international stars. They have been offered a number of other exciting gigs, including one from Las Vegas. One way or another, Spelbound will definitely be seeing their name in lights!

Britain's Got Talent Tour:
Spelbound spent three weeks performing on the *Britain's Got Talent* live tour, with the other stars of the show. It was great fun for them, as they got the chance to perform for some of the people who voted for them, and had a taste of the fame and publicity to come.

Victory Parade:
After they won the competition, the delighted group toured Staines and Ashford in an open-topped bus. Hundreds of people lined the streets to wave, cheer and get autographed photos. The group posed for photos and signed autographs, then went on to meet the Mayor.

Royal Variety Performance:
As well as the £100,000 prize money, Spelbound has won a once-in-a-lifetime chance to appear at the Royal Variety Performance. They are determined to put together a routine that will enthral and delight the Royal Family.

Olympic Dreams:
As Amanda pointed out during the final, Spelbound's mesmerising act would be a fantastic opening act for the 2012 Olympics. They hope that their popularity will help to get acrobatic gymnastics in the Games for the first time.

1ST BRITAIN'S GOT TALENT PLACE

SERIES 1 MEMORABLE

The first series of *Britain's Got Talent* gave the UK a huge, healthy dose of family entertainment.

Connie Talbot melted everyone's heart with her beautiful singing voice.

Bessie Cursons may not have won, but she is surely destined for a career on stage.

The Bar Wizards delighted the audience with their flair for bartending!

Tony Laf's singing won the hearts of the audience.

The baton-twirling Craig Womersley got a standing ovation from the crowd.

MOMENTS

Cheeky Bits lit up the stage with their exuberant dancing!

Young Dominic Smith impressed the Judges and the audience with his exceptional voice.

Young dancers Luke and Charlotte were a firm favourite.

The first winner of *Britain's Got Talent* Paul Potts set a high standard for all future finalists.

The Kombat Breakers fused breakdance and street with eye-popping results.

SERIES 2 MEMORABLE

Audiences couldn't wait for the new series of *Britain's Got Talent* to begin, and people were queuing up to show off their weird and wonderful talents.

Charlie Green wowed Simon Cowell with his singing.

Donald Bell Gam gave an unforgettable performance!

Signature's inspired and unique act embodied fun and entertainment!

Beautiful belly dancer Sophie Mei gave a dazzling performance.

Freestyle footballer Jeremy Lynch displayed incredible ball-control skills.

The Cheeky Monkeys brought a smile to everyone's face.

The judges didn't like Alex's singing, but they loved his flair for comedy!

Craig Harper has been entertaining since he was eight and definitely has the likeability factor.

Bang On made music out of anything they could lay their hands on!

George Sampson's dance skills took him all the way to the Royal Variety Performance!

SERIES 3 MEMORABLE

Series three took Britain by storm and catapulted Susan Boyle to international fame. It just goes to show, *Britain's Got Talent* can do anything!

Body popper Aidan Davis brought energy and passion to the stage.

Five-year-old magician Tom Herron drew gasps of amazement with his act.

Super-talented Callum Francis will surely see his name in lights one day.

The Dreambears pulled out spangles and high kicks to impress the Judges.

Darth Jackson – postal worker by day, terror of the galaxy by night!

Everyone was singing DJ Talent's catchy song!

Breakdancing pensioner Fred Bowers won the hearts of the audience.

James Boyd's failed record attempt has gone down in *Britain's Got Talent* history!

Stavros Flatley were an unlikely but fantastic dancing sensation!

One song changed Shaheen's Jafargholi's life.

103

SUSAN BOYLE

"Susan, you are a little tiger.

AMAZING AUDITION

Susan Boyle's first jaw-dropping audition has reached legendary status. Smiles flitted across the faces of audience and Judges alike as the quietly spoken lady stepped onto the stage. No one guessed that they were about to witness true magic. Her voice brought people to their feet and gasps of astonishment and wonder were heard all around the theatre. Where had this amazing talent sprung from? No one could believe their ears.

"You are one special lady."

"It was a complete privilege listening to that."

UNEXPECTED FAME

Thanks to the power of the Internet, word of Susan's incredible audition spread around the globe. Her name was on everyone's lips, and TV stations from all over the world were camping out on her street, hoping for an interview. By the time the semi-finals began, the pressure on Susan was intense. But she stayed calm and sang her way to the *Britain's Got Talent* final.

"When I step on that stage it's an accumulation of forty years of dreaming."

WHAT HAPPENED NEXT?

Since becoming runner-up in *Britain's Got Talent*, Susan Boyle has had a spectacular year. It's all been like a dream come true for the lady from West Lothian in Scotland. She has achieved a lifelong ambition and released an album in 2009, which has won critical acclaim.

Susan Boyle has become a one-woman global sensation, with hundreds of millions of YouTube hits, and interviews on numerous UK and American TV shows. Her story is an inspiration. It reminds us all that if you pursue your dreams with determination, fearlessness and hope, anything is possible. Fairy tales are made of this.

★ Series 3 Winner ★

DIVERSITY

"Utterly, utterly fantastic."

EXPLOSIVE AUDITION

A love of dance brought the eleven members of Diversity together, and that passion lit up the stage of *Britain's Got Talent* last year. Their audition was spectacular and surprising. It was immediately obvious that this act was something special.

"Sheer and utter perfection."

"I've never seen dance so imaginative, so creative, so entertaining."

"Incredibly creative."

GLITTERING FINAL

Nerves were jangling before the all-important final. The group's dreams rested on this performance. They were determined to give it their all. They moved as if they shared one body, leaping and springing across the stage and drawing cheers and gasps from the audience.

The exciting, comical and inventive choreography brought the crowd to its feet. At last, Dec announced that Diversity had won, and a world of opportunity opened up in front of them!

"It was dynamic, it was funny, it was imaginative – superb."

WHAT HAPPENED NEXT?

Diversity's appearance on the Royal Variety Performance will remain one of the highlights of their careers. They threw themselves wholeheartedly into creating a routine that would impress the Queen – and be a thank you to all the people who had voted for them. Since winning *Britain's Got Talent*, Diversity has been nominated in the Dance section of the final South Bank Show awards and won an accolade at the Pride of Britain awards.

They have become Patrons of Dance Aid, performed at the Wireless Festival in Hyde Park and appeared in a Michael Jackson tribute at the Winter Gardens in Blackpool. They have even performed outside 10 Downing Street. Diversity's 2010 UK tour has been massively popular and their career looks set to go from strength to strength!

WINNER 2011

WINNER?

1. KNOW YOUR STUFF

Whatever your act, make sure that you know it inside out and back to front. Nerves can make your mind go totally blank when you're on the stage, so you need to know your routine like the back of your hand.

2. PRACTICE MAKES PERFECT

Plenty of rehearsal is important to make a really good impression. Take some time every day to practice, but don't overdo it. Resting should be a part of your preparation too!

3. LIKE YOUR ACT

If you're singing or dancing to music, pick a tune that you really love. Your enthusiasm and enjoyment will come across to the audience and the Judges.

4. BRING BACKUP

If you're singing, prepare a second song. If you've watched the auditions before, you'll know that sometimes the Judges ask an act to perform something different.

5. BARE NECESSITIES

You're bound to get hungry and thirsty, so bring a bottle of water and some sandwiches to keep you going.

6. DRESS THE PART

Think carefully about your outfit. You'll want to make an impression, but it'll be a long day and you need to feel fresh and comfortable for your audition. Choose something that you feel happy in – something that suits your personality.

7. BE FRIENDLY

There will be lots of people waiting to rehearse, and they'll understand better than anyone how you're feeling. Chat to them and maybe you'll make some new friends!

8. PREPARATION IS VITAL

It's really important to warm up before you go onstage. Whether you're singing, dancing or doing something completely different, you need to be prepared to perform.

9. SMILE

The Judges and the audience like to see a happy, open face, so try to swallow your nerves and give them a dazzling smile when you walk onstage!

10. BELIEVE IN YOURSELF

Have faith in your abilities and your talents, and pour your energy and enthusiasm into your performance.